HOUGHTON MIFFLIN HARCOURT

JOURNEYS

Road Map to Success

Write-In Reader
Grade 1 Vol. 2

Printed in the U.S.A.

ISBN: 978-0-547-25404-3

56789 -0877- 17 16 15 14 13 12 11 10

4500249765 B C D E F

HOUGHTON MIFFLIN HARCOURT
School Publishers

Contents

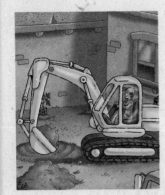

✓ **WORDS TO KNOW**

around

because

before

light

Outer Space

Complete the sentence. Check the best word.

1 It lets off smoke _the_ it is hot.

☐ because   ☑ around

2 He set up his flag _the_ he left.

☑ light   ☐ before

3 Green rings spin _the_ it.

☑ around   ☐ before

4 This man felt as _the_ as dust.

☑ because   ☐ light

Read the words in the word box.
Write the word under the picture.

hose	note
robe	rose

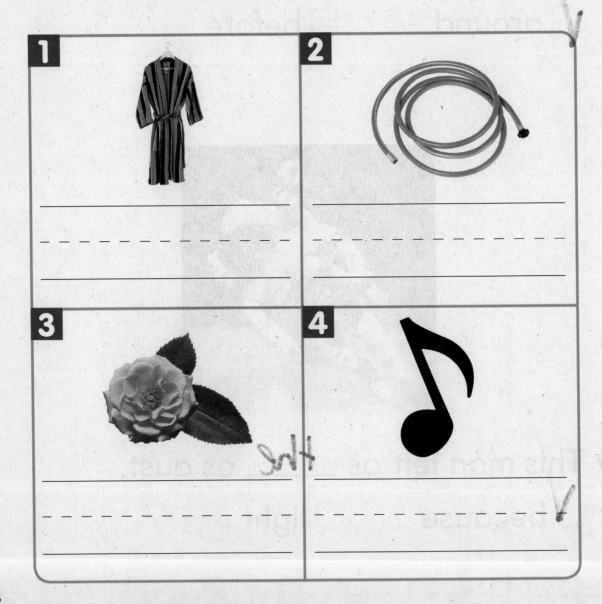

1.

2.

3.

4.

Bo's Big Space Trip

by Megan Linke

Bo sat in his space ship.

He set its knobs and switches.

"Space trip!" yelled Bo. "Go, go, go!"

But his mom said, "Lunch time!"

5

Little Bo had big plans.

He had his map.

"Space trip!" yelled Bo. "Go, go, go!"

But his mom said, "Bed time!"

"Rest, Bo," said Mom.
"Rest **before** you go."
"OK," said Bo. "If I must."

Then Bo rose up, up, up!

His ship puffed smoke.

Bo felt as **light** as dust!

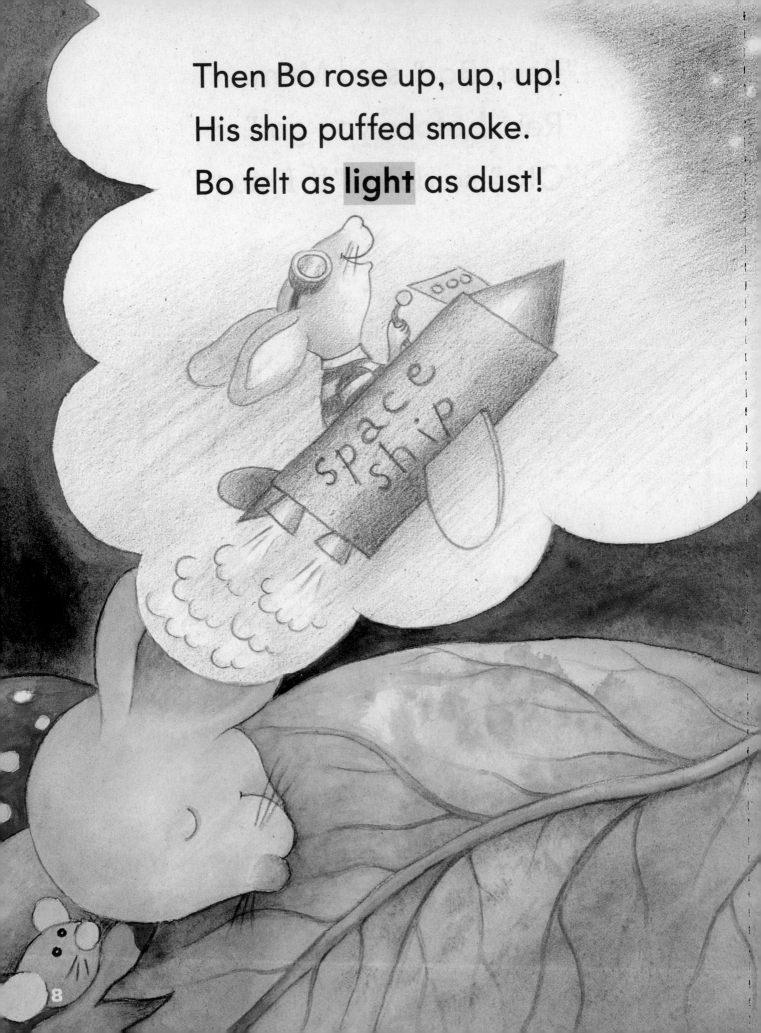

Huge dots lit up all **around** him.

Bo felt little **because** space was so big.

Little Bo missed his mom.

Then Bo woke up.

He gave his mom a hug.

"Space is fun," said Bo.

"But I am glad to be home."

Check the answer.

1 What is the main idea of this story?

☑ Little Bo wants to go to space.

☐ Little Bo has a map.

2 What does Bo's space ship have?

☑ stars   ☑ switches

3 Check a detail from Bo's trip.

☐ Bo has glasses on.

☑ Bo's mom comes with him.

Write about Bo's trip.

4 Did Bo really go to space?

the lihtg

✓ **WORDS TO KNOW**

by

car

don't

sure

Let's Go on a Trip

Complete the sentence.

Check the best word.

1 We can go ____ bus.

☐ by ☐ car

2 That bike slips, so ____ take it.

☐ don't ☐ by

3 Let's go in Dad's _____.

☐ sure ☐ car

4 I am _____ we will not be late!

☐ don't ☐ sure

Read the words in the word box.
Write the word under the picture.

beak	**bee**
seat	**feet**

1.

2.

3.

4.

14

 Pops   Rex   Lee   Ace   Pink

Pops Takes a Trip

by Marc Vargas

Pops sat in his **car**.

"Here I go!" he said.

"Can I go?" asked Rex.

"OK," said Pops.

"Be **sure** you **don't** sit on Lee."

Lee did not speak.

He just said, "Squeak."

"Me, me!" yelled Ace.

"This will be fun!"

So Ace got in back.

Clunk! Bang! Clank!

Pink got in as well.

"No seat for me?" asked Pops.

"Must I go **by** bike?"

"Yup!" said Rex.

Then Pink made space.

"Sit by me, Pops!" she said.

"Thanks, Pink," said Pops.
And off they went.
Beep! Beep! Beep!

Check the answer.

1 **Who has the car?**

☑ Ace ☐ Pops

2 **What sounds does Ace make in the car?**

☐ clunk, bang, clank

☑ beep, beep, beep

3 **Who makes space for Pops?**

☑ Rex ☐ Pink

Write about a place you went.

4 I went to ___the vind___ .

Lesson 18

✓ **WORDS TO KNOW**

first

sometimes

these

under

Let's Eat!

Complete the sentence.
Check the best word.

1. Eat lots of _the_ grains.

   ☐ first   ☐ these

2. Kay eats sweets _the_.

   ☐ sometimes   ☐ under

the wind

3 Amy's place mat is ___the___ her plate.

☐ these   ☐ under

4 Ray drinks his milk ___th___ at each meal.

☐ these   ☐ first

Write a Word

Read the words in the word box.
Write the word under the picture.

pail	pay
snail	rain

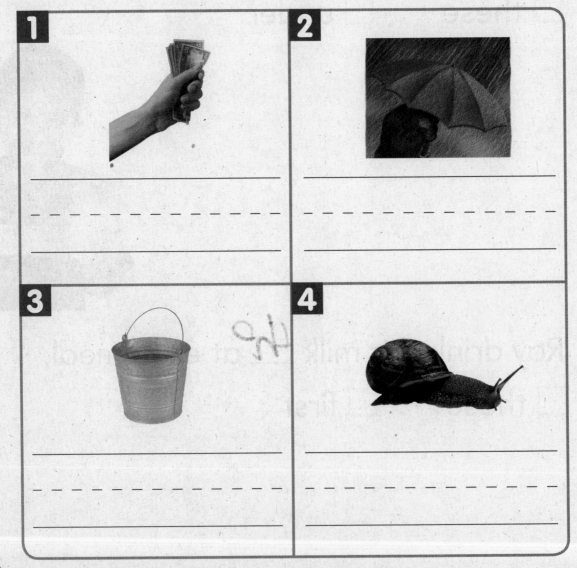

1

2

3

4

Ant's Grand Feast

by Megan Linke

Seats got kicked back.

And kids left to play.

But they did not clean up.

This is my day!

An ant can eat lots.

So **first** let me say,

I can eat, eat, eat, eat,

Each week and each day.

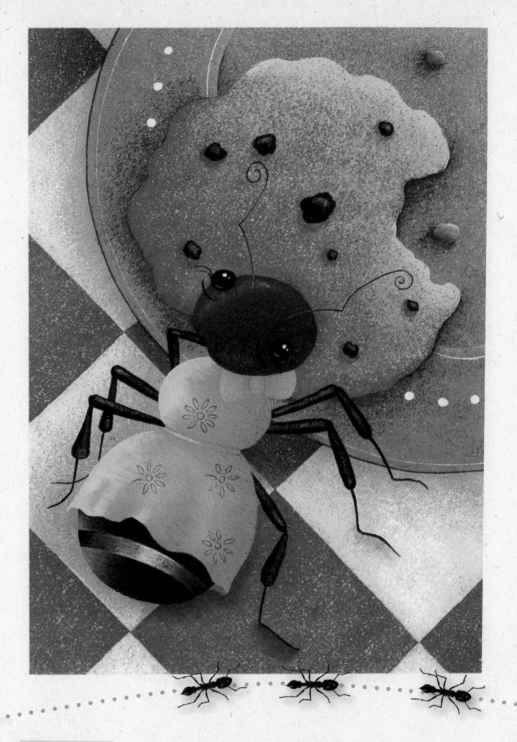

These crumbs may be trash.

But as we can see,

Sometimes trash is a feast,

For an ant such as me!

See this? It's still fresh!

It sat **under** that plate.

It's as big as I am,

But I will eat it. Just wait!

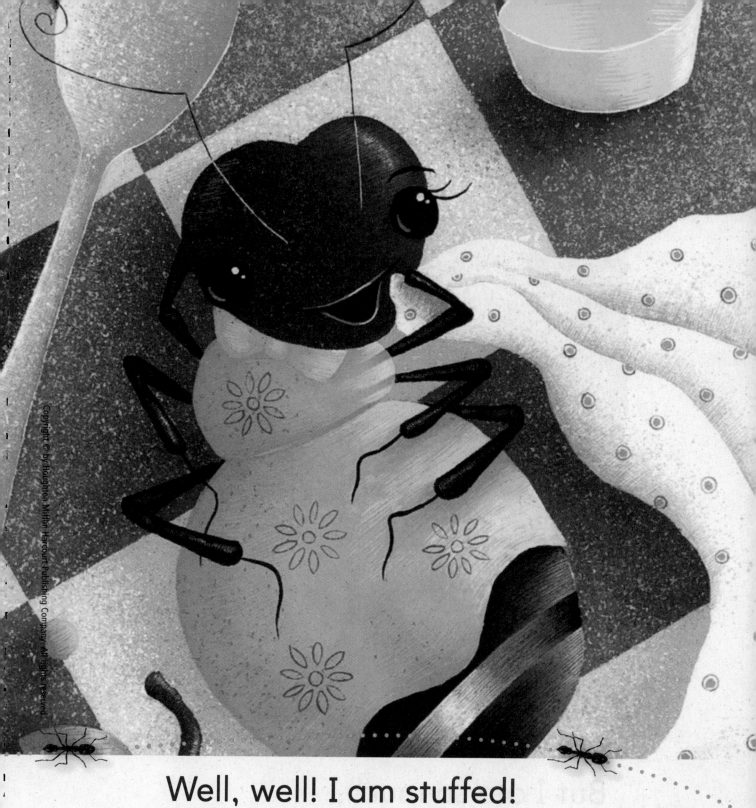

Well, well! I am stuffed!

I am too stuffed to think,

But I wish that I had

Just a little to drink.

But I ate so much,
And I am in such pain!
So I think I will stay here
And wait till it rains.

Check the answer.

1 Why was this story written?

☐ for fun

☑ to teach us what to eat

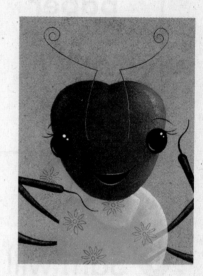

2 How was this story told?

☐ only in pictures

☑ in rhymes and pictures

3 In the end, why does Ant rest?

☑ She is full.   ☑ She is scared.

Write about your favorite food.

4 I like to eat _____.

WORDS TO KNOW ✓

great

paper

soon

work

When We Grow Up

Complete the sentence.

Check the best word.

1 Sam will make a _____ vet.

☐ paper ☐ great

2 Joan will _____ at home like Dad.

☐ work ☐ soon

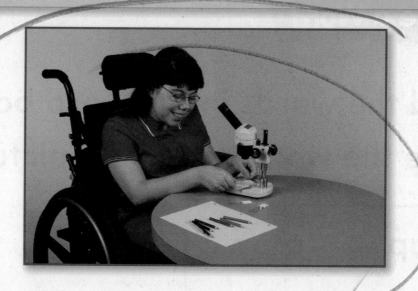

3 Jane will take notes on ___.

☐ great ☐ paper

4 We will grow up ___!

☐ soon ☐ work

Write a Word

Read the words in the word box.
Write the word under the picture.

> soap   crow
>
> boat   snow

1

2

3

4

When Tom Grows Up

by Diane Bird

Tom sat on his mom's knee.

"When I grow up," said Tom,

"I will write like this. I will paint, too!"

Each day, Tom did his spelling drills.

But he did not moan and groan.

He could not wait to write.

Then Tom got a paint set as a gift.

Tom glowed. "This is **great**!" he said.

He picked up some **paper**.

Tom painted and painted.

He showed his paintings to his pals.

"This is not bad," his pals said.

Tom had set his goal.

He had to **work** at it.

But he did not quit.

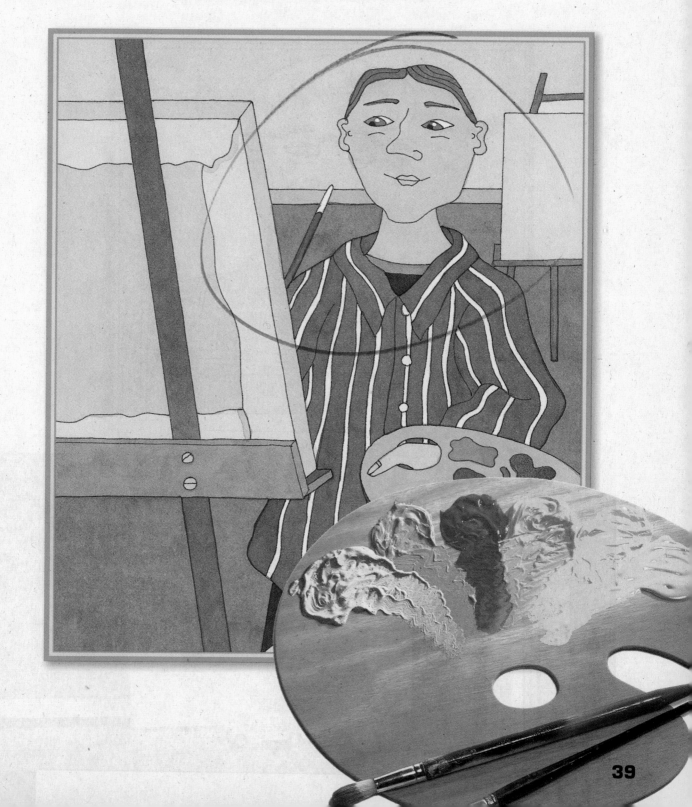

Tom's work **soon** paid off.

These days, Tom writes for kids.

And he paints for them, too!

Check the answer.

1 **What does Tom want to do?**

☐ teach kids ☐ write stories

2 **When does Tom make up his mind?**

☐ as a kid ☐ as a grownup

3 **What made Tom want to write?**

☐ His friend told him to write.

☐ His mom read him stories.

Write about yourself.

4 **What will you be when you grow up?**

_____

_____

Nature

more

old

try

want

**Complete the sentence.
Check the best word.**

1 This tree is very _____.

☐ old ☐ more

2 The foxes will _____ to find food.

☐ more ☐ try

③ It will pick up _____ pinecones.

☐ more ☐ try

④ We _____ to keep this place clean!

☐ old ☐ want

Read the words in the word box.
Write the word under the picture.

peanut   mailbox

seashell   sailboat

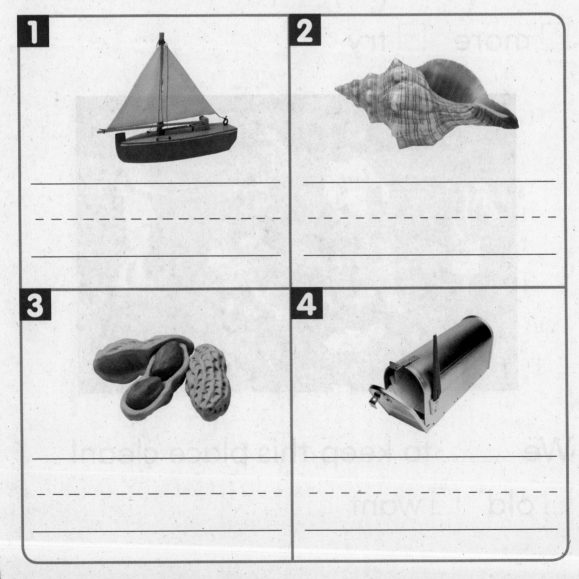

Tree Frog Sings His Song

by Megan Linke

In the **old** days, Tree Frog was glad.

He sang and sang, all day long.

"Jip-jip, croak!" he sang. "Jip-jip, croak!"

Tree Frog did not have many fans.

"He thinks he can sing!" said Duck.

"What a joke," buzzed Bug.

At last, Duck made him stop.

"Quit singing!" Duck said.

"No one likes that song."

Tree Frog was crushed.

Tree Frog hid himself in his tree.

Then a face came and peeked at him.

"Hush," she said. "**Try** and cheer up."

"I cannot," Tree Frog sniffed.

"No one likes my song."

"I like it!" said his new pal.

"I **want** you to sing **more**."

At that, Tree Frog jumped up.

These days Tree Frog sings at sunset.

And he is as glad as can be.

Check the answer.

1 Why did Duck talk to Tree Frog?

☐ to tell him to quit singing

☐ to tell him he should sing

2 How did Duck make Tree Frog feel?

☐ very sad

☐ angry

3 What made Tree Frog happy?

☐ The moon liked his song.

☐ Duck said, "I'm sorry."

Write about Tree Frog's new pal.

_____

4 She is _____.

✓ **WORDS TO KNOW**

pretty

saw

thought

told

These Trees!

Complete the sentence.
Check the best word.

1 Sam _____ trees were fun.

☐ pretty   ☐ thought

2 This tree has _____ thick bark.

☐ pretty   ☐ thought

3 We _____ a tree with red leaves.

☐ saw ☐ told

4 Dad _____ me how to plant a tree.

☐ saw ☐ told

Read the words in the word box.
Write the word under the picture.

star	jar
yarn	shark

1

_____

- - - - - - - - - - -

_____

2

_____

- - - - - - - - - - -

_____

3

_____

- - - - - - - - - - -

_____

4

_____

- - - - - - - - - - -

_____

321 Park Street

by Paulo Rizzi

I was born at 321 Park Street.

"Park" was an odd name for it.

It was not much like a park.

Parks need trees!

I **thought** we needed trees as well.

Trees can be such fun to swing in.

And on hot days, trees can make shade.

So at last, I spoke with Landlord Jake.

I **told** him we needed trees.

He said, "Find trees, Jim.

Then you can plant them."

So I did it! I had my pals help me.

We had fun planting those trees.

But it takes time for trees to grow.

That part made me sad.

At sunset, we **saw** a big truck drive up.

Landlord Jake came with it.

"Nice job, kid," he said.

"This is a gift for your hard work!"

These days, it is **pretty** nice in this yard.

I like swinging in my tree's branches.

And on hot days, there is lots of shade.

Look Back and Respond

Check the answer.

1 **Where does this story take place?**

☐ by Jim's home ☐ on a farm

2 **Who are the main characters?**

☐ a tree and a building

☐ Jim and Landlord Jake

3 **Why does Jim get sad?**

☐ He never gets any trees.

☐ Trees take a long time to grow.

Write about Landlord Jake's gift.

4 His gift is _____

_____.

✓ WORDS TO KNOW

baby
follow
learning
until

Birds of a Feather

Complete the sentence.

Check the best word.

① This crane glides _____ it needs rest.

☐ until ☐ follow

② The little ducks _____ their mom.

☐ until ☐ follow

3 A mother bird feeds her _____.
☐ baby   ☐ learning

4 This chick is _____ to feed itself.
☐ baby   ☐ learning

Read the words in the word box.
Write the word under the picture.

bird	dirt
fern	nurse

1

2

3

4

Peacock and Crane

by Megan Linke

One day, Peacock met Crane.

"I feel bad for you," chirped Peacock.

"Being dull and gray is such a bore."

It was not a nice thing for him to say.

But Crane did not feel hurt.

"I am fine being this way," said Crane.

"Is that so?" asked Peacock.

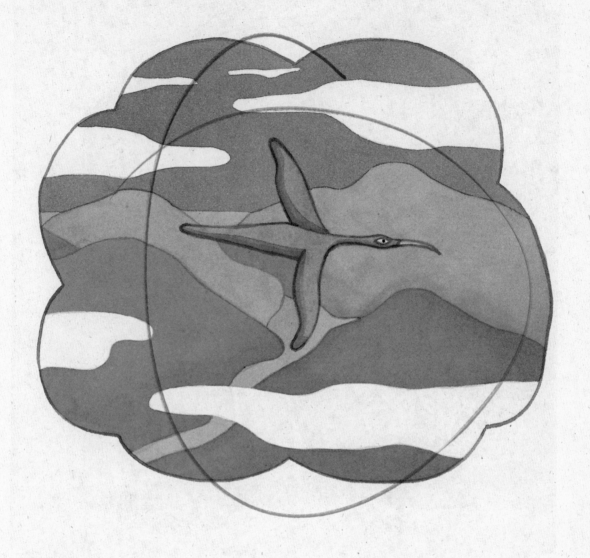

"Yes, it is!" said Crane. "See this?
Cranes can glide for miles and miles."
Crane spread his long wings.
He whirled and turned in the wind.

It seemed like such fun!

Peacock wished he could **follow** Crane.

He beat his wings **until** he lifted off.

But he did not glide like Crane did.

"I first did this as a **baby**," said Crane.

"**Learning** it was not hard.

You are quite pretty, Peacock.

But you will never glide like me."

Peacock sat thinking.

For the first time in his life, he got it.

All birds were gifted, not just him!

Each bird was great in its own way.

Check the answer.

1 **Which word best describes Peacock?**

☐ proud   ☐ funny

2 **What can Crane do?**

☐ glide   ☐ puff up

3 **What lesson does Peacock learn?**

☐ how to fly for miles

☐ that all birds are special

Write about yourself.

4 **What makes you special?**

_____

—————————————————————————————

_____

Pet Pals

again
began
nothing
together

Complete the sentence.
Check the best word.

① Their dog Chip ___ to run.

☐ began   ☐ together

② Brook and her cat sat ___.

☐ nothing   ☐ together

3 Max has ___ in his bowl.

☐ nothing ☐ again

4 Shane fed her fish ___.

☐ began ☐ again

Read the words in the word box.
Write the word under the picture.

woods	book
cook	hook

1 _____

2 _____

3 _____

4 _____

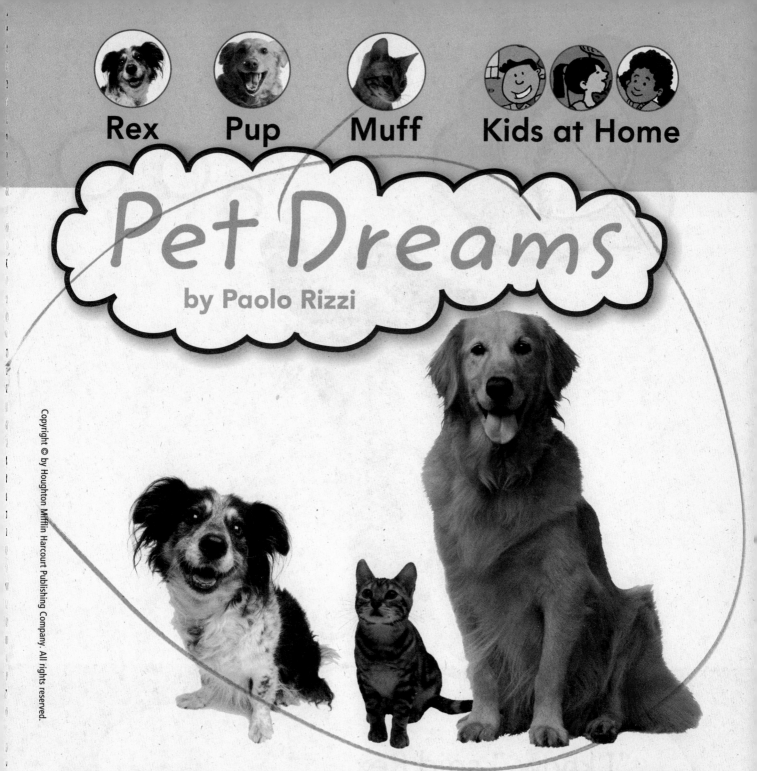

Rex Pup Muff Kids at Home

Pet Dreams
by Paolo Rizzi

Rex, Muff, and Pup sat dreaming **together**.

"Being a pet is such a bore," Muff said.

"The kid at my home is just no fun."

Muff shook her head.

"I know," said Rex.
"The kid at my home just plays catch.
Back and forth, time and **again**!"

"If he'd just chase things with me,"
Rex said, "that would be good!"

"Yes, **nothing** beats hunting," said Muff.

"My kid just tosses fake mice.

That is no fun.

I wish she'd go bird hunting with me!"

"What I hate," said Pup, "is bath time.
If I could just take mud baths!
That would be good."

Just then, dinner bells **began** ringing.

At that, Muff stood up.

"Woof, woof!" yelled Rex and Pup.

And the pets all ran off home.

Look Back and Respond

Read Together

Check the answer.

1 Why is Rex mad at his owner?

☐ His owner just plays catch.

☐ His owner chases chipmunks.

2 What does Pup want in his bath?

☐ mud ☐ soap

3 What makes the pets go home?

☐ dinner bells ringing

☐ their owners calling

Write about the pets' dreams.

4 _____

_____

Butterflies

WORDS TO KNOW

anything

kind

upon

warm

Complete the sentence.
Check the best word.

1 It is nice and _____ in the sun.

☐ warm ☐ kind

2 This _____ of insect has big wings.

☐ kind ☐ warm

3 It sits _____ a leaf.

☐ anything ☐ upon

4 Is _____ inside it?

☐ upon ☐ anything

Read the words in the word box.
Write the word under the picture.

moon	spoon
boot	screw

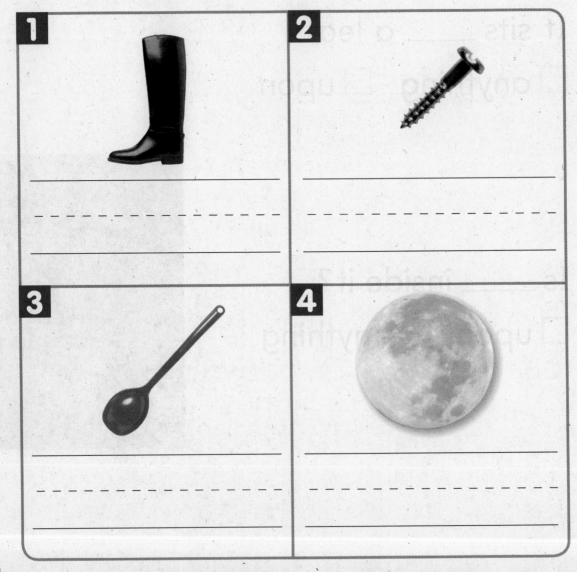

1

2

3

4

The Things You Can Find

by Megan Linke

One **warm** spring day, Ant set off.

Soon she saw an odd thing.

"What have we here?" she asked.

Then she stuffed it in her bag.

Next, Ant marched under a bench.

A few crumbs fell down.

Ant scooped them up.

She stuffed them in her bag.

"Hum, hum," said Ant.
"What next?"
She looked up at an odd green thing.

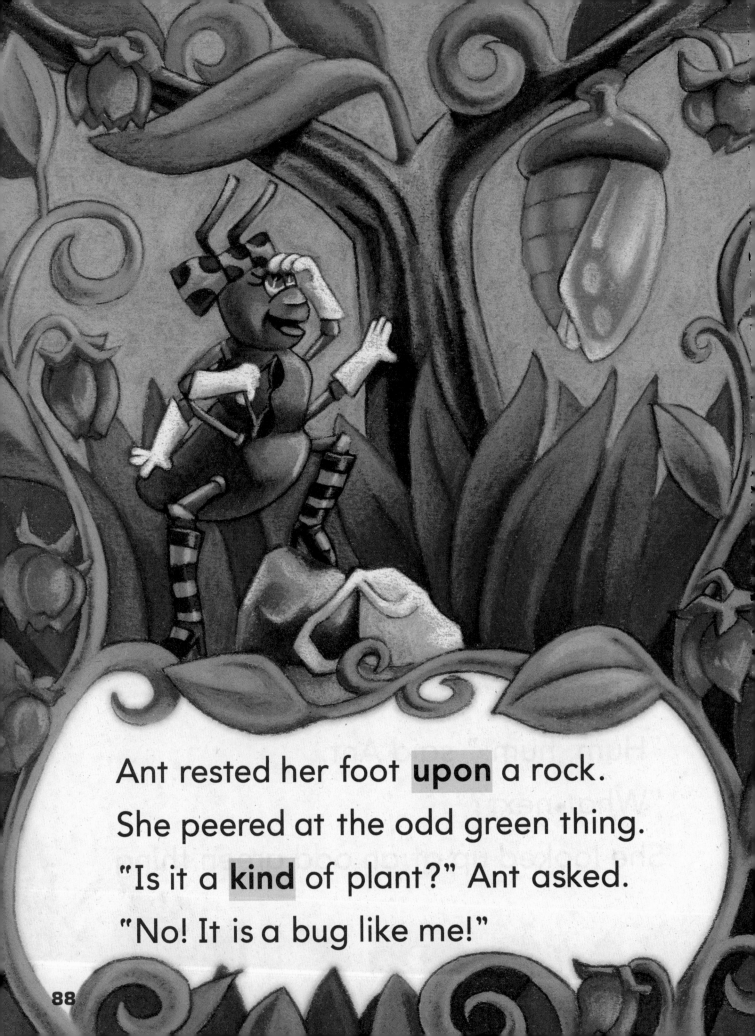

Ant rested her foot **upon** a rock.
She peered at the odd green thing.
"Is it a **kind** of plant?" Ant asked.
"No! It is a bug like me!"

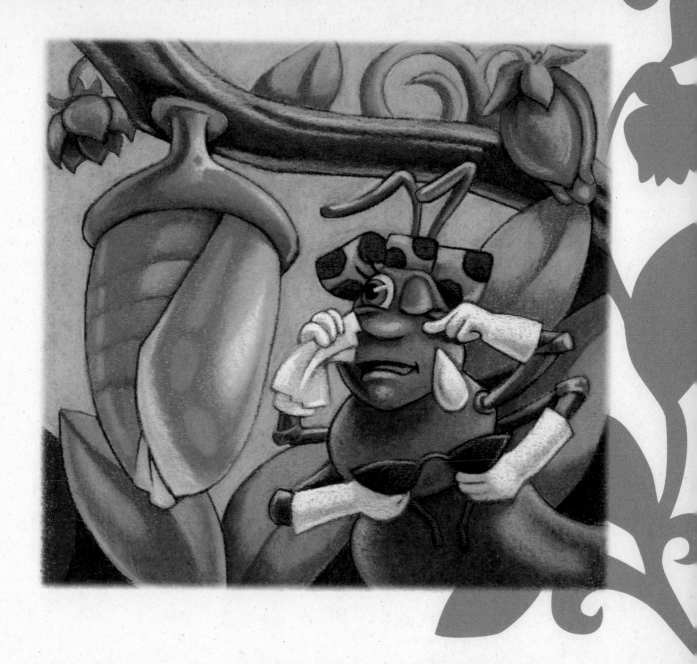

"I am sad for you bug," sniffed Ant.

"You cannot run and jump.

You cannot do **anything**!"

"Not true!" said the thing, and it shook.

Then it spread its wings and took off.

Ant just shook her head.

"Well, well!" she said.

"The things you can find!"

Check the answer.

1 What did Ant find first?

☐ the noodle ☑ the crumbs

2 What did Ant find last?

☐ the green thing ☐ the noodle

3 What happened last?

☐ The thing turned into a butterfly.

☐ Crumbs dropped on Ant.

Write about the green thing.

4 _____

✓ **WORDS TO KNOW**

buy
family
myself
please

Moving Day

Complete the sentence.
Check the best word.

1. A new _____ will live next door.
   ☐ family ☐ buy

2. I will _____ them a gift.
   ☐ family ☐ buy

3 Can you _____ help lift this box?

☐ myself ☐ please

4 I cannot pick it up by _____.

☐ myself ☐ please

Write a Word

Read the words in the word box.
Write the word under the picture.

cow   owl

couch   cloud

1 _____

2 _____

3 _____

4 _____

Who Will It Be?

by Marvin Hampton

Raccoon went out to sweep his step.

As he swept, a big truck drove up.

"Did an animal **buy** that house?" he asked.

"Who will it be?"

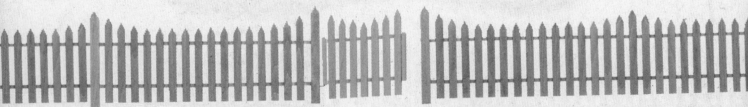

"I hope it's not a crab," thought Raccoon.
"Crabs are quite proud and not too nice.
Crabs can pinch, too!"

"Maybe it will be an ox.

An ox may stomp on my plants.

An ox may stomp on me!

I will need to hide **myself** inside."

"It may be a frog.
Frogs are quite loud.
Frogs ribbit and ribbit and ribbit.
Dear me, I hope it's not a frog!"

"Perhaps it will be clams.

Clams are not much fun.

I cannot invite clams for tea."

Just then, Hen and her **family** showed up.

Raccoon saw nothing wrong with hens.

"Nice to meet you!" shouted Raccoon.

"**Please** stop by for tea one day!"

Check the answer.

1 How does Raccoon feel at the beginning?

☐ worried   ☐ excited

2 Why doesn't Raccoon like frogs?

☐ Frogs are loud.   ☐ Frogs are mean.

3 Why doesn't Raccoon like clams?

☐ Clams are not much fun.

☐ Clams make too much tea.

Write about Raccoon.

_____

4 Raccoon is _____.

✓ **WORDS TO KNOW**

even

studied

surprised

teacher

Art Class

Complete the sentence. Check the best word.

1 My art _____ is very nice.

☐ even ☐ teacher

2 I made it _____ better by adding blue.

☐ even ☐ teacher

3 Sol _____ each marker.

☐ surprised ☐ studied

4 I _____ my mom with a gift!

☐ surprised ☐ studied

Write a Word

Read the words in the word box.
Write the word under the picture.

napping	spotted
smiling	striped

1

_____

- - - - - - - - - - - -

_____

2

_____

- - - - - - - - - - - -

_____

3

_____

- - - - - - - - - - - -

_____

4

_____

- - - - - - - - - - - -

_____

Dog-Print Art

by Janice Winfield

It was raining.

Henry and I had nothing to do.

We were bored, bored, bored.

I got out paints and paper.
But then my pal Jenny **surprised** me.
"Are you ready, Jill?" she asked.
"Let's go shopping!"

Shopping put me in a good mood.

But when we got back, that ended.

Footprints! Nose prints!

Dog prints on that nice clean paper!

Henry's red nose gave him away.

At first I got really mad.

Then I **studied** Henry's art close up.

I picked up Henry's painting.
I added dots and lines.
"It was not bad," I told him.
"But now it will be **even** better."

Mom thought so, too.

And Mom's an art **teacher**, so she knows!

After that, my good mood came back.

Not bad for a rainy day!

Check the answer.

1 How are Jill and Henry the same?

☐ They both paint.

☐ They are both always bored.

2 What does Jill do with Henry's art?

☐ throws it out ☐ makes it better

3 Jill's mood gets _____ by the end.

☐ better ☐ worse

Write about a rainy day.

4 _____

- -

Our Talents

Complete the sentence.

Check the best word.

1 Sue tells the funniest ____.

☐ stories   ☐ different

2 We are all good at ____ things.

☐ always   ☐ different

3. Painting makes Britt _____.

☐ happy   ☐ stories

4. Pam _____ wins at checkers.

☐ happy   ☐ always

Read the words in the word box.
Write the word under the picture.

| happy | happier |
| messy | messier |

1

_____

- - - - - - - - - - - - -

_____

2

_____

- - - - - - - - - - - - -

_____

3

_____

- - - - - - - - - - - - -

_____

4

_____

- - - - - - - - - - - - -

_____

What Can You Do?

by Megan Linke

My pal Sammy tells jokes.

His **stories** are great.

Sam is the funniest kid!

He's much funnier than Kate.

Kate can't tell jokes.
She blows bubbles instead!
That Kate can blow bubbles
As big as her head.

I wish mine got like that,
But that's not my thing.
What I am good at is singing.
I can sing like a king!

My pal Sally is smart.
She does math like a pro.
She can add and subtract
Ten times better than Jo.

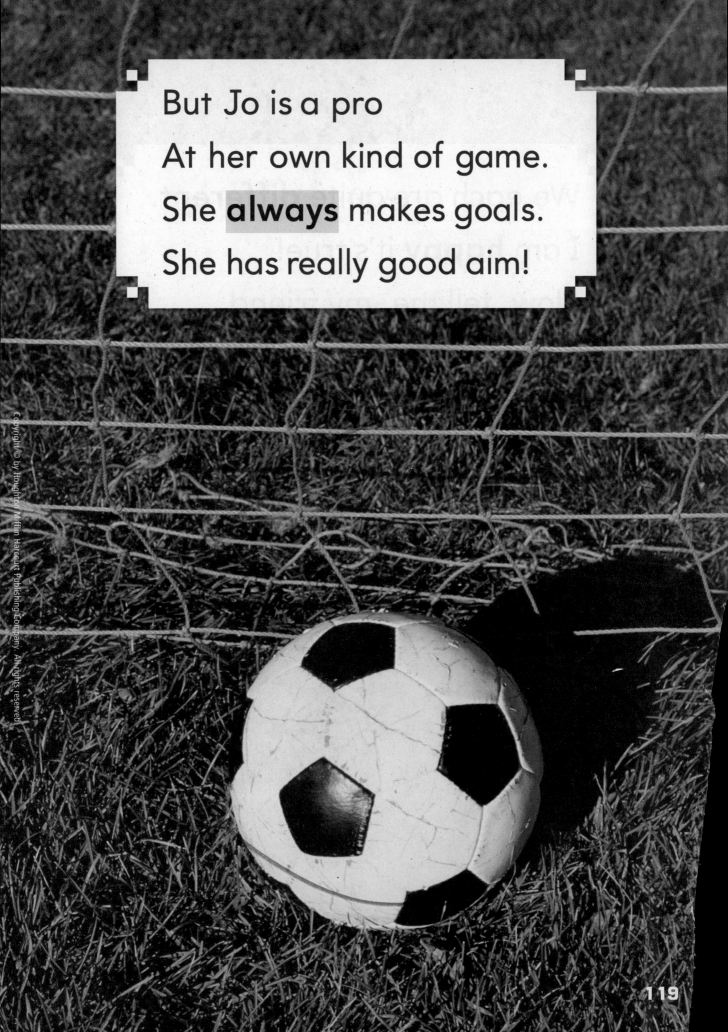

But Jo is a pro
At her own kind of game.
She **always** makes goals.
She has really good aim!

We each are quite **different**.
I am **happy** it's true!
Now, tell me, my friend,
Tell me, what can you do?

Check the answer.

1 **What is special about this story?**

☐ It rhymes.

☐ It has no words.

2 **What is page 115 about?**

☐ telling jokes

☐ playing soccer

3 **Why are there numbers on page 118?**

☐ to teach us math

☐ because the words are about math

Write about your own special skill.

4 _____

_____

✓ WORDS TO KNOW

cried
heard
large
should

I Can Do It!

**Complete the sentence.
Check the best word.**

1 We can lift this ____ box.

☐ large ☐ cried

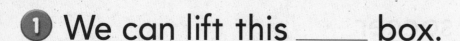

2 "I win!" she ____.

☐ heard ☐ cried

3 Mom and Dad _____ me singing.

☐ heard ☐ should

4 You _____ try out for the team!

☐ should ☐ large

Read the words in the word box.
Write the word under the picture.

light	pie
night	cry

1

_____

- - - - - - - - - - - - -

_____

2

_____

- - - - - - - - - - - - -

_____

3

_____

- - - - - - - - - - - - -

_____

4

_____

- - - - - - - - - - - - -

_____

Mighty Little Mole

by Paolo Rizzi

One day, Mule came upon an odd thing.

"Why, this looks like food!" said Mule.

"How nice!"

Mule grabbed it and tugged.
But the **large** thing was stuck tight.

"I cannot pick it up by myself," said Mule.

So Pig came up to help him.

"We **should** tie this rope on," said Pig.

Mole **heard** them crying.

"Can I help?" he asked.

"Don't be silly," grunted Mule.

"You are too little," gasped Pig.

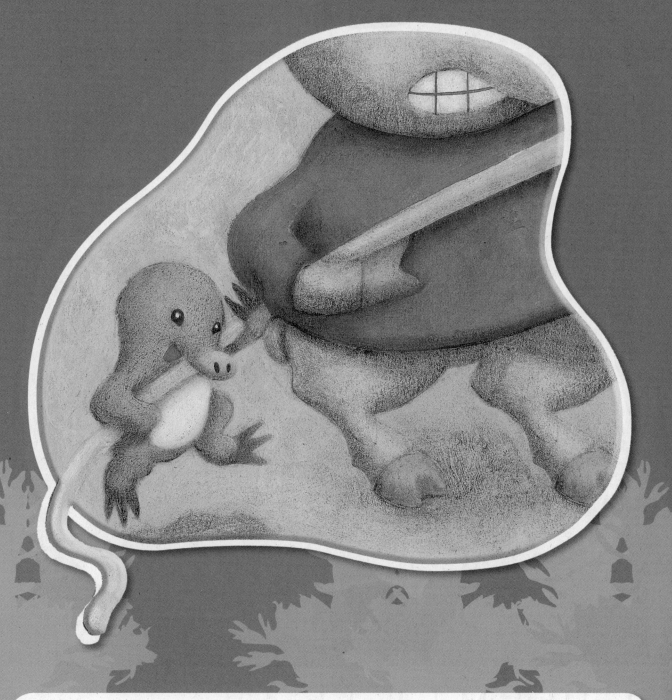

But Mole had to try.

He grabbed the rope.

He tugged with all his might.

Pop! Little Mole had done it!

"Mighty Mole to the rescue!" yelled Mule.

"Dinner at my place!" **cried** Mole.

Look Back and Respond

Check the answer.

1 Who are the characters in this story?

☐ Mule, Pig, and Mole

☐ a carrot and a piece of rope

2 Where does this story take place?

☐ at Mole's house   ☐ outside

3 What is Mule's problem?

☐ He cannot get the carrot out.

☐ He has no friends.

Write about Mole.

4 Mole is _____

_____ .

Interesting Insects

Complete the sentence.
Check the best word.

1 Can you see the bug in the _____?

☐ gone   ☐ leaves

2 It will fly away.
Soon it will be _____.

☐ gone   ☐ almost

3. The praying mantis is _____ done eating.

☐ almost   ☐ idea

4. What will it do next? I have an _##_.

☐ idea   ☑ leaves

Read the words in the word box.
Write the word under the picture.

helpful	sunny
playful	quickly

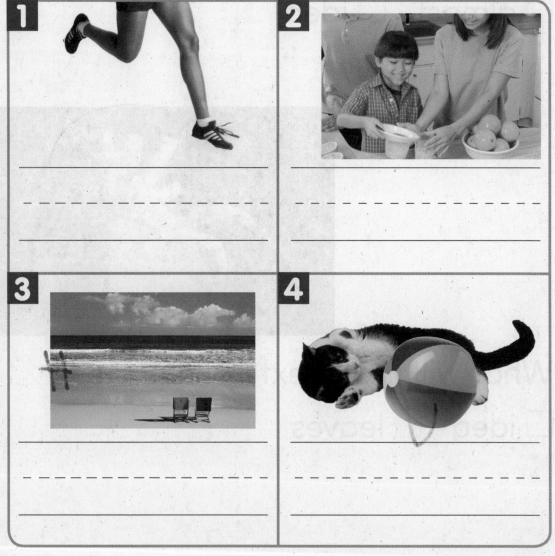

1 _____

2 _____

3 _____

4 _____

Stick Bug's Awful Idea
by Paolo Rizzi

Stick Bug sat happily munching an apple.

He stopped when he felt a drop.

Drip, drop, trickle, drop!

Water fell quickly from the **leaves**.

"This cannot be rain," said Stick Bug.

"It is a sunny day!"

Then Stick Bug got an **idea**.

"What if the sun is melting?" he cried.

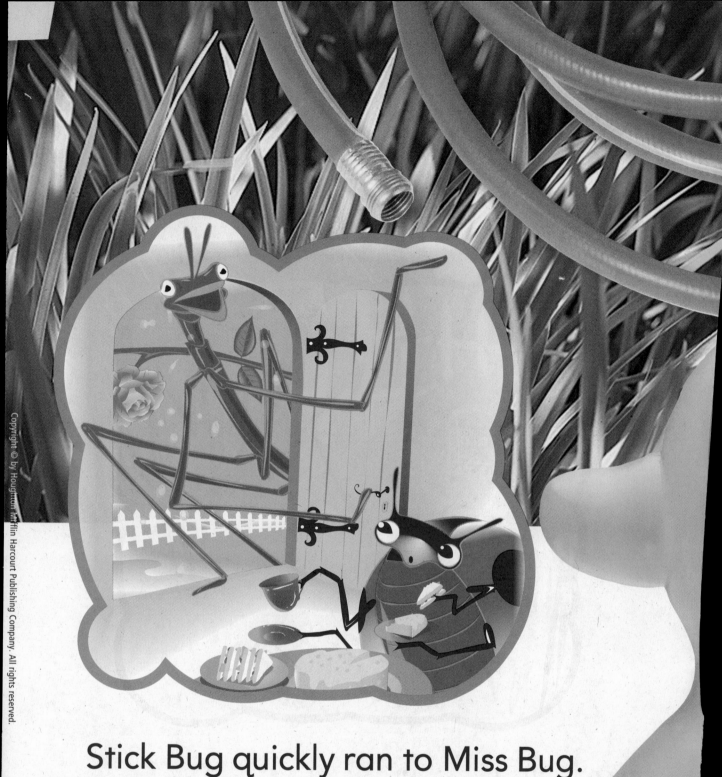

Stick Bug quickly ran to Miss Bug.

"Miss Bug!" he yelled loudly.

"The sun is melting!

It will soon be **gone**!"

"We will drown!" cried Miss Bug.

Then she ran to tell Ant.

"The sun is melting!" Miss Bug shouted.

"It is **almost** gone!"

The three bugs ran to tell Mommy Ant.

But Mommy Ant did not shout or cry.

"Look up, my little insects," she said.

"The sky is blue," said Mommy Ant.
"The sun is still shining brightly.
It was just time to water the plants!"

Check the answer.

1 Why did Stick Bug stop eating?

☐ He felt water.

☐ Miss Bug told him to stop.

2 How did Stick Bug make Miss Bug feel?

☐ happy   ☐ worried

3 Who told Stick Bug what really happened?

☐ a man   ☐ Mommy Ant

Write about your favorite kind of bug.

4 _____

_ _

_____

✓ **WORDS TO KNOW**

everyone

field

loved

most

Kick It!

Complete the sentence.
Check the best word.

1 The players ran up the _____.

☐ everyone ☐ field

2 Our team plays _____ days.

☐ most ☐ loved

3 When she scored, _____ cheered.

☐ everyone ☐ field

4 They _____ being part of a team.

☐ loved ☐ most

Write a Word

Read the words in the word box.
Write the word under the picture.

music	open
baby	donut

1

_____

- - - - - - - - - - - -

_____

2

_____

- - - - - - - - - - - -

_____

3

_____

- - - - - - - - - - - -

_____

4

_____

- - - - - - - - - - - -

_____

Soccer Sisters

by Roberto Gómez

Edith and Meg both **loved** soccer.

Most times, this was a good thing.

But not always.

One day, Mom was driving them home.

Meg's team had just played.

"You played so well, Meg!" said Edith.

"I hope I can play like that on Friday!"

Meg stopped smiling.

"You are playing on Friday?" she asked.

"I am too! You'll be playing my team!"

From then on, the sisters were not pals.

"I can run faster than you!" growled Edith.

"I can kick harder than you!" growled Meg.

On the big day, Edith ran up the **field**.

Pow! When she scored, **everyone** cheered.

Meg cheered as well.

She even forgot that she was mad.

"You know," said Meg,
"It does not matter who wins.
Playing with you is so much fun."
"I think so, too," said Edith. "Let's play!"

Check the answer.

1 **How are Edith and Meg related?**

☐ They are sisters.

☐ They are cousins.

2 **Why did Edith and Meg get upset?**

☐ They had to stop playing soccer.

☐ They had to play against each other.

3 **Why did Meg forget she was mad?**

☐ The game ended.

☐ Edith made a goal.

Write about your favorite sport.

4 _____

_____

PHOTO CREDITS